A great
brother
Thank you
for your
support.
Be blessed

MY QUEEN, VOL. 2
THE SONG OF JORDAN BROWN

**Black Queen, Precious Jewel,
I Sing for You**

BY ISSOUFOU OUATTARA

© YAHWEH BANK STUDIO

WWW.YAHWEHBANK.ORG

Preface

As a poet, I have always been fascinated by balladeers and other singing poets. This is certainly why I created the fictional character called, "JORDAN BROWN," as one of the characters of the collection of love poems "My Queen".

This collection helps me to express myself about the matters of love and life which are essential for my being. Who can live without love?

In this book entitled: "Black Queen, Precious Jewel, I Sing for Thee." I wish to celebrate the beauty of black women not as a political tool to deny others their beauty, but simply as a way to honor them.

So I dedicate this volume to all black women and other women around the world.

Love is the true bread of life. This is why we shall not be shy to magnify it. May the readers enjoy the book.

The author

Issoufou Ouattara

I Sing for you

The sun rises

In the east,

The morning is beautiful.

My words are yours

O black Queen

O precious jewel

I sing for you.

I stretched my glance

To the corners

Of the earth.

I looked in the North,

I looked in the south

I looked in the east

And in the west.

But, I found

Nowhere a match

For the queen of queens.

You are marvelous,

You are beautiful,

You are the dream

Of ten thousand bards.

O black Queen,

O precious jewel,

I sing for you,

I sing for you.

Your Crown

I have seen

Your crown

Glimmer in the splendor

Of the day.

I too dream of you.

O beautiful one,

O you with the eyes

Of a dove,

And the glamor

Of a gorgeous night

Full of the lustful

Aroma of love.

Come to me,

    O beauty of my dreams.

Come to me

    O flower full of passion.

Make me not wait

    Too long,

To celebrate the lovely

    Seduction

Of the evening

    By your side.

Let the silhouette

    Of your splendor

Carry me away

In your tender world.

Let me be yours for once

To boast the sweet

Taste of your love...

O my precious lady.

O lovely queen,

O my delicate flower,

I dream of you.

I dream of you.

The sight of you

At the fall

Of the sun,

I saw you pass by

And the glamour

Of your beauty

Captured my soul.

Like a smooth dancer

I saw you walk along

The path of my glance.

But who do you walk for,

So magnificently,

Like a splendid kite

In the sky

Of an innocent heart?

I have seen you steal

My heart with the resplendence

Of your gorgeous beauty.

I am here,

O my queen...

I am here to venerate

The seduction of two.

If you have been

Seeking for love

You have found it.

So wait no more

O my dear lady,

    O my lovely queen,

Come to meet the desire

Of my heart.

    At the fall of the sun

    I saw you pass by

And the glamour

    Of your beauty

Captured my soul.

You are a queen...

You are a beautiful

Black queen.

Seduction

Seduce me

With your words.

Seduce me

With your voice.

O you beautiful one,

I have walked

The streets of the city

To search for your love.

To find your voice.

But, are you with me?

Yes, are you with me?

The joy of a poet

Is the song

> Of his beloved dove.

You are my peace.

> You are my love.

I am as worthy as

> You judge me to be.

So seduce me

> With your words.

Seduce me

> With your voice.

I am made for you;

> I am made for you.

O my lovely jewel.

You are here

I hear

The moaning

Of our hearts

    Which are captured

By the power of our love.

Embrass me

    Even stronger.

For I love the sweet

    And smooth caress

Of your presence.

    You are tender

Like a soft wind

That refreshes

The soul of one who travels

Across the desert.

You were gone,

But now you are here...

And I melt in your hands.

O my sweet love,

O my sweet queen.

Dance with me

Dance with me,

O my dear lady.

Dance with me,

O sweet love.

I will sing a song

For you

From the lyre of my heart.

I will bring forth

The sweetest of melodies

For the joy of being with you

And the happiness that I gain

From your presence

In my days and nights.

So dance with me,

O my sweet darling,

O my sweet queen.

For when the night falls,

I wait for your calls

To enjoy the moment

Of a lovely dream

By your side.

So dance with me,

O my sweet black queen.

Like a rainbow

Like a rainbow breaks

Into beautiful colors,

So I have seen the beauty

Of your love in my favor.

To what may I compare you?

O my lovely daisy,

O my sweet lily!

I will compare you

To a flower that is planted

In the rich soil

Of a royal garden.

You are precious

O my dear lady.

You are the pearl

That causes travelors

To cross the sea.

So come to me,

O precious one.

So come to me.

And let us be one.

The roads I traveled

These roads

I traveled alone,

Pondering when

The day will come

So that I can enjoy

A moment

Of abundant love

By your side.

Yes, my darling,

I have been here,

Secretly keeping

My best love

For you alone.

O my beloved,

O my sweet black queen,

I seek for love

In no other place

But from your heart.

Let it be so,

O my sweet lady.

Let it be so,

O my sweet darling,

Since I can't live

Without you.

When the night falls

When the night falls,

I will go by the river side

Where the wind is fresh

And the grass is soft and green.

I will come there

To write ten thousands

Verses to celebrate

The beauty of our love.

The gist of the matter

Is that I love you

More than ever.

So my dear lady

Come and let me

    Desire the deepness

Of your love.

    You are worth

The dream

    Of a million bards.

pen your heart

Open your heart

O my beloved queen,

So that I can boast

The sweetness

Of your lovely soul.

Open your heart,

O my sweet black lily.

I have waited so long

To see you be mine.

Where have you

Been hiding your love?

I am so lonely without you.

I am so cold without

Your warmth.

But when the morning comes

    I will sing for you

Like a balladeer.

I am the balladeer

Who sings for your heart...

    When the evening comes,

You will still inspired

The sweetest of my dreams.

I think of you all the time,

    I dream of you,

O my lovely darling.

So come to satisfy the desire

Of my lonely heart.

Yes, my lovely daisy

My sweet tulip

Rose of my dreams,

Come to capture my heart

For the glorious promise

Of a solemn day during which

I shall open my mouth,

To boast about

The sweetness

Of your beautiful love.

I traveled

I traveled

In the city of your heart

And tasted the abundance

Of its sweetness.

"Am I dreaming?"

I asked myself.

"I am dreaming?"

Your world is so wonderful;

Your world is so beautiful.

O my sweet lady,

I traveled in the city

Of your heart

And I failed not to put on paper

Few verses to honor

Your greatness.

O my sweet lady,

If I ever forget to praise you

In the midst of crowds

Let my reputation

Be covered with shame.

For a lady like you

Deserves the best of words

That a lover can offer.

I traveled

The city of your heart

And I saw the beauty

Of its abundance.

So before all people I confess

That neither gold nor money

Will ever replace my love

For my sweet darling.

Yes, I traveled

In the city of your heart

And tasted the abundance

Of its sweetness...

So my sweet black queen,

You shall always be mine.

If I shall die

If I shall die,

Let it be

For your sweet love.

If I shall fall

In the cruels ditches

Of a battlefield,

Let it be the battlefield

Of your heart.

A queen like you

Is worth the tears

Of the mightiest man.

I was a mighty

Man once;

But, now I am weak

Before your love.

This is sweet,

This is sweet to my soul.

If I shall die

Let it be for

Your sweet love;

O my sweet one,

O my sweet Queen.

Some songs

Some songs

Are better when

They are not sung alone.

So let my voice praise

Your love.

What is a lover's life

If the seduction

Of his beloved lady

Does not cause him to sing

For her heart.

O my darling,

I need you by my side.

Don't go away from me.

But instead, keep me

In the warmth

Of your loving heart.

Some songs

Are better when

They are not sung alone.

But I wonder if you

Will be mine;

O my beautiful queen

O my lovely flower,

Let me be with you

Again.

I will dive

I will dive in the beauty

Of your compassionate

Heart and bring forth

Ten thousand verses of love

Made for the seduction

Of your heart

And the admiration

Of your splendor.

So come,

O my beloved,

So Come,

O sweet love unthamed.

Tonight, when the stars

Of the sky have gathered

To inspire the hearts

Of lovers,

I too shall gladly

Be stealing yours.

A woman like you

Is worth a million verses

And even more.

Rasputina

Rasputina,

The bad lady

Has come to steal

The love that I have

For my beloved queen.

She stood on my way

And tempted me

As much as she could.

I did not fall for her;

I did not betray my love

For my beloved;

I did not deny my love

For my sweet flower.

    Rasputina,

The wicked woman

    Has come to steal

The love that I have

    For my beloved flower.

But she is not

    The one that I desire.

Sometimes

Sometimes,

One plus one

Equals one...

You and I are one,

O my dear lady,

O my lovely one...

Sometimes,

One plus one

Equals one.

This is the nature

Of love and passion.

I have been away

For a short time,

    For a long time

I should say.

O gosh,

    Do you know

How much

    I miss you.

Sometimes

    One plus one

Equals one.

    Because

We are made

    To be one.

Your beautiful smile

A beautiful smile

On your face;

A lovely look that makes me

Dream of far away lands.

There is no one like you.

I saw you walk by,

O you lovely queen...

How could I forget

Your beautiful ways

That forshadowed the lovely gift

Of a lovely night by your side.

I dream of a wedding day,

For you and I.

O my lovely lady,

O my beautiful one.

I see a pretty smile

On your face,

A lovely look

That makes me dream of you.

I want to be yours...

I dream to be yours.

Come again in my dreams

O you,

O you,

Beautiful black queen.

Bright dreams

Bright dreams,

Full of hope.

Bright dreams and a

Lovely walk in the dark

Days of my past.

I saw your love...

Your beautiful love

That touched my soul.

But where are you?

O my sweet darling!

But where are you?

I miss you so much.

Bright dreams

That I keep secret

For my beautiful queen.

Come to me,

When you can.

You walked by

...and you walked by,

O you,

With the lovely face,

When shall I marry you

And enjoy the gift

Of your beautiful seduction.

I have closed my eyes,

To dream about you.

But when I open them

Will you be here with me.

O beautiful queen who enchants

My lonely nights.

One day

One day maybe,

I shall be happy

To have you as a spouse.

O my lovely queen,

O my beautiful jewel.

For some of us,

Roses are made

For a holy purpose.

So in the precious comfort

Of a church's room

Where you shall dragged

Your overflowing wedding dress,

I will lift up my head

To heavens to say thank you

For the gift of your love.

One day maybe,

I shall be happy

To have you as a spouse.

And dream again

With you by my side.

Thank you

O my lovely one,

Thank you

For your love.

O my sweet lady,

There is no one like you.

With you by my side,

I can now boast merry days.

Thank you

O my beloved

For your precious

Gift of love.

If the weather is beautiful

If the weather

Is beautiful

I will walk outside.

Do you remember

The park where

You and I used to go?

I heard that its grass

Is green again...

Being with you

Is always

A special moment

For me.

So if the weather

    Is beautiful,

I will walk outside

    To our meeting place

Where the grass

    Is always green.

Will you be there?

    Will you be there

    Once again

For the celebration

    Of our love?

A splendid flower

A splendid flower

Stands a few steps

Away from me.

A plendid flower

That enchants my solitary heart.

Good morming

My dear queen!

Good morning,

Black Lily!

When it pleases your heart

To look for a lover

Would you consider mine?

Black tulip

Black tulip,

Gorgeous smile,

Lovely face,

You sat by my side,

Quietly and beautifully.

So I gather all my bravery

To speak with you.

But I fail again.

To measure up

To your splendor.

Black tulip, gorgeous queen,

I love your ways.

When she was Gone

When my lady was gone;

My heart is broken.

I was seen here and there

Asking for help from

Passers by.

But my beloved one,

Came back to me.

When my lady was gone;

My heart was broken.

So I have cried to God,

And He healed me

With her return.

Will you be mine?

A red rose,

Beautiful indeed...

A red rose,

Standing ahead of me.

O my lady,

You are lovely

Like the sunrise

By the side

Of Niagara Falls.

You are a river of life,

That feeds the admiration

Of a multitude

With its sparkling beauty

And gorgeous eyes.

A red rose, you are.

A beautiful rose indeed.

But will you

Be mine?

The gateway of Eden

The gateway

Of Eden

Is closed,

Once and forever,

How can I see

My beloved lady?

Yes, the doorway

To love is locked

Like a treasure

Is kept in banks.

Destiny has purposely

Ajourned the mating

Of our minds.

Like a blind man in darkness,

    I seek your way

    O my lovely queen.

    But the gateway

To Eden is closed...

Yet, I have not lost

My faith in God

Who can can open

    The door for me.

Beautiful love

Beautiful love

In the street

Of my dreams.

Beautiful love

That I wish to capture.

O you,

My sweet lady,

Do you know the song

Of my heart?

I am the prince

Of love and peace;

I am the ruler of the moon.

The stars know my name.

They move for me.

I am the bard

Of good fortune.

So come to me,

O beautiful one.

To offer me

The gift of a lovely night...

O beautiful love

In the street

Of my dreams.

How I dream

To hold you again.

I am blind

I am blind

To myself

And the good things

That I have.

I am blind

To myself

But not

To your love.

One day,

I will marry you.

One day,

We will be one.

I am blind

    To myself

And to the good things

    That I have.

But I will never be

    Blind to your love.

O my dear queen,

    O my sweet darling...

My queen

My queen,

I will bring you

A rose from

    A far away land

Where the morning

    Is beautiful

And the evening

    As well.

My queen,

    Your words

Are beautiful

    Like the seduction

Of the wind

On the grassland

Of tropical savannahs.

The morning

Compares not

To the freshness

Of your gentleness.

Yes, my queen,

You are marvelous,

Like a dove

In a field of wild flowers.

My queen,

Come to me,

I am the prince of love.

I am the gift of peace.

From my mouth

Come forth

Beautiful words

In favor of thee.

O my queen,

You are lovely,

You are beautiful

Like the glamour

Of a lovely day

In the best

Of spring gardens.

Silent night,

Silent night,

I took my pen

To write for you.

You are my queen,

You are a jewel...

A woman like you

Is a gift from heavens...

I am grateful

For your love.

I am grateful

For your beauty...

Silent night

Silent night

I took my pen

To write for you...

Because you are a queen...

Because you are

A beautiful

Black queen...